◤ A MATERIAL WORLD ◥

It's
METAL

KAY DAVIES and WENDY OLDFIELD

Wayland

A MATERIAL WORLD

It's Glass   It's Plastic
It's Metal   It's Wood

Editor: Joanna Housley
Designer: Loraine Hayes

First published in 1992 by
Wayland (Publishers) Ltd
61 Western Road, Hove
East Sussex BN3 1JD, England

British Library Cataloguing in Publication Data
Davies, Kay
It's metal. – (A material world)
I. Title II. Oldfield, Wendy III. Series
669

ISBN 0 7502 0362 5

Typeset by Kalligraphic Design Ltd,
Horley, Surrey
Printed and bound in Belgium by Casterman S.A.

Words that appear in **bold** in the text are
explained in the glossary on page 22.

IT'S METAL

If you look around, you will see lots of things made from metal. There are many different types of metal, and this book will show you what they are used for. We obtain metals like iron, gold and copper from under the ground. We can then use them for practical objects like bridges, or valuable things like jewellery. Gold is a very precious metal. It is rare and beautiful. Steel is very hard, and used for large, strong structures. In this book, you will learn all about these and many other uses of metal in the world today.

Each metal has its own special colour.
Some metals are shiny and hard.
They can be made into many
beautiful and useful things.

Aluminium cans keep drinks fresh and fizzy. When they are empty we drop them in the bin.

They can be **recycled** to make new objects from the metal.

You may have seen some of these kitchen tools. They are made from metal because it can be strong and sharp. Do you know what the tools are used for?

Can you see all the metal dishes in this restaurant kitchen?

We use metal pots and pans for cooking because they heat up quickly and help cook our food.

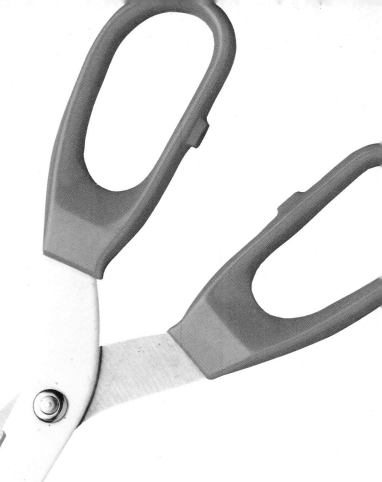

The sharp edges of
scissors help us
cut carefully.

The handles
help to make
them safe and
easy to use.

Magnets are made of iron and steel. They pull some metals towards them. How many paperclips are hanging from this magnet?

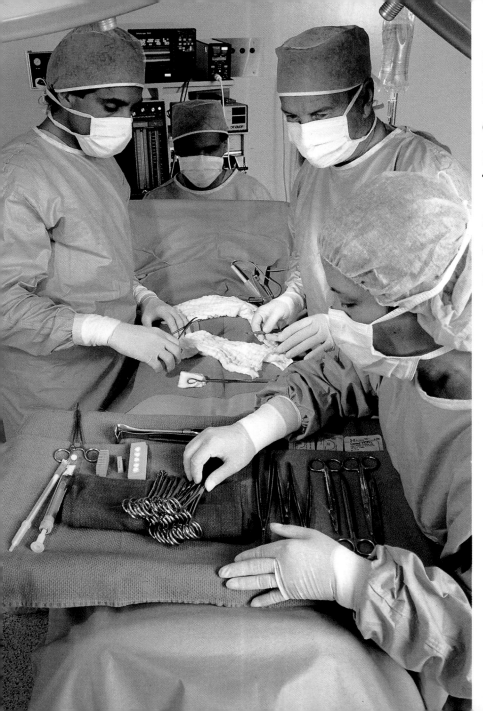

Doctors use metal **instruments** in operations to make people better. Their smooth surfaces can be cleaned and used again.

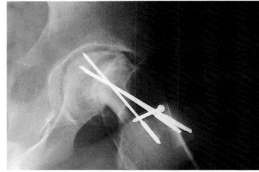

Strong metal pins hold broken bones together while they mend.

The weight-lifter pushes heavy metal weights high into the air.

He practises hard and tries to lift more weights each time.

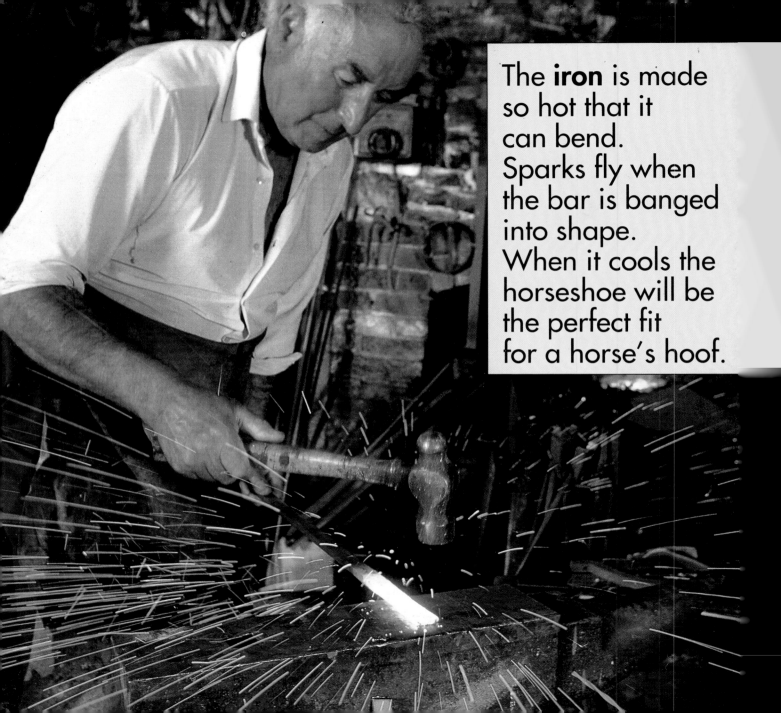

The **iron** is made
so hot that it
can bend.
Sparks fly when
the bar is banged
into shape.
When it cools the
horseshoe will be
the perfect fit
for a horse's hoof.

Each little
piece in a
clock fits in
with the others
like a jigsaw.
The **cogs** move
round together
to turn the
hands of
the clock.

13

The boy can bounce and spin and do clever tricks on his bicycle.

The wheels and the hollow tubes of metal in the frame are strong enough to take his weight.

The train has a smooth shape to help it go fast.

It carries passengers safely over long distances. Its wheels follow metal tracks as it speeds along.

This musical instrument is a saxophone. It is made from a metal called brass.

The man can make music when he blows through it. We can listen or dance to its music.

Gold is a rare and valuable metal that lasts for ever. These golden domes glitter in the sunshine. They make an important place look very beautiful.

Steel bridges carry traffic over rivers.

The wind blowing through the metal **girders** cannot push the bridges down.

It is exciting
to find old
metal objects
in the soil.

Thousands of
years ago this
bronze shield
protected
someone in
battle.

19

The old car looks sad and worn. Once its paint shone and it worked well.

Now its iron body is **rusting** in the air and rain.

Scrap metal is piled high in the yard. It will be melted down and new things made from the old junk.

GLOSSARY

Aluminium A hard, light, silvery-white metal.

Bronze A brownish metal made from copper and tin.

Cogs Wheels with teeth on their edges. They fit and turn together.

Girders Steel beams used to hold up heavy loads.

Instrument A tool, such as a knife used by a doctor, or an object that can be played to produce musical sounds.

Iron A silvery-white, shiny metal.

Recycled Made into something new instead of being thrown away.

Rusting The effect of air and rain on iron which weakens it and wears it away.

Shield A piece of armour to protect the body.

Steel A hard, strong and long-lasting metal made from iron.

BOOKS TO READ

Resources Control by Alexander Peckham, (Franklin Watts, 1990)

I Wonder How Steel is Made by Neil Curtis (Heinemann Children's Reference, 1990)

Recycling Metal by Joy Palmer, (Franklin Watts, 1990)

Some books in the following series may also be useful:

Simple Science (A & C Black)

Starting Science (Wayland)

TOPIC WEB

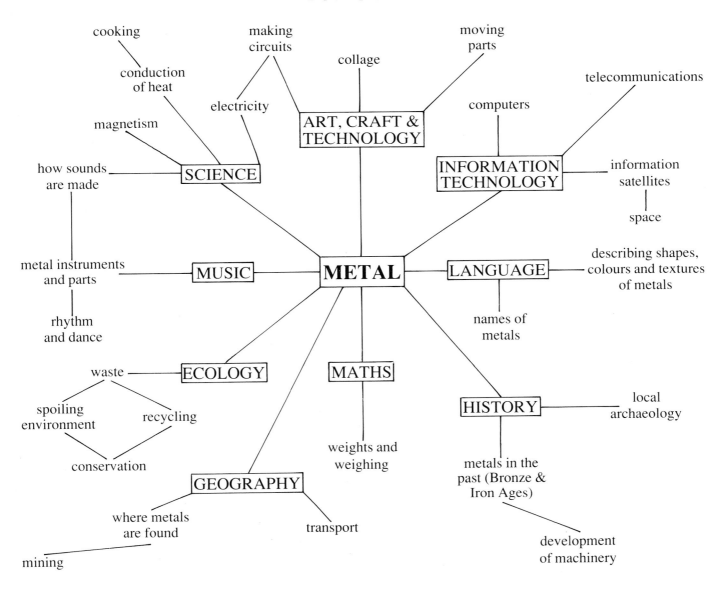

cooking

making circuits

moving parts

conduction of heat

collage

telecommunications

magnetism

electricity

computers

how sounds are made

SCIENCE

ART, CRAFT & TECHNOLOGY

INFORMATION TECHNOLOGY

information satellites

space

metal instruments and parts

MUSIC

METAL

LANGUAGE

describing shapes, colours and textures of metals

rhythm and dance

names of metals

waste

ECOLOGY

MATHS

spoiling environment

recycling

HISTORY

local archaeology

conservation

weights and weighing

metals in the past (Bronze & Iron Ages)

GEOGRAPHY

where metals are found

transport

development of machinery

mining

23

INDEX

Picture acknowledgements

Chapel Studios 8 (inset), 13; Eye Ubiquitous cover (top, Paul Seheult), 6 (Paul Seheult), 8 (main pic, Paul Seheult), 18 (Judyth Platt), 20 (Geoff Redmayne), 21 (Dave Fobister); St Mary's Hospital 10 (inset); Tony Stone Worldwide cover (left), 4, 10 (main pic), 12 (Rob Talbot), 14, 17 (Douglas Armand); Wayland Picture Library 7 (Michael Dent), 9 (Zul Mukhida), 15, 19 (British Museum); ZEFA 5, 11, 16.